It was
that
one
moment

# It was
# that
# one
# moment

Dan Hughes' poetry and reflections
on a life of making relationships with children,
young people and their families

DAN HUGHES, Ph.D.

worthpublishing.com

First published 2012 by Worth Publishing Ltd.
worthpublishing.com

Printed by CPI Group (UK) Ltd, Croydon CR0 4YY

British Library Cataloguing in Publication Data
A catalogue record for this book is available from the British Library

ISBN  9781903269213

Cover and text design: Anna Murphy

This book is written for my own family,
as well as for each child and
for each family I have journeyed with

# Contents

**INTRODUCTION**      ix

**A BROKEN BEGINNING**      1

Lying among the stones      5

So hard to be a child      8

invisible      11

Shame      14

I will not listen to your lies      17

There must be other children      19

The hardest      23

If my parents had died      27

I want my own      30


**A SECOND START**      35

You ask why I act as I do      38

In our eyes      41

A prayer of an abused child  (recently adopted)      47

Let me go with you  (from a therapist)      54

Who am I?  (from an adoptive mother)      59

Your sweet persistence      67

I wanted a mom      70

Remembering my father      74

This one child                                      78

The belly laugh                                     81

Gratitude to an old groundhog                       85

Dancing in the light                                87

I love you                                          91


**INTERSUBJECTIVITY**                               **97**

Your moving words                                   101

With clarity and joy                                103

Moments of psychotherapy and
    similar relationships                           105

I will play                                         108

Talking moments                                     110

Being a kid                                         113

Here-and-now-together                               116

One-of-a-kind                                       119

Intersubjectivity                                   121


**GLOSSARY**                                        **124**

**REFERENCES**                                      **127**

# Introduction

I am a therapist. A therapist for children. For children who have been hurt. Hurt by their parents through action or through the lack of action.

I am also a therapist for the new parents of these children, parents who are struggling to care for their son or daughter, although the child may be struggling not to be cared for. Sometimes these parents are foster parents (as they are known in the US) or foster carers (as they are known in the UK). Sometimes they are adoptive parents. Sometimes these new parents are actually the original parents who hurt the children. They are now willing and able to care for their children, but their children may not be willing and able to now respond to their care.

Being a therapist for children who have experienced abuse, neglect, and abandonment means that I must enter their experiences. Enter the terror, the shame, the despair, and the rage that these children have experienced alone, often for years. I must strive to understand their experiences. In doing so, I must first accept – truly accept – that these children have actually experienced these difficult-to-think-about events. Then I must strive – truly strive – to understand how the child experienced those events, though every aspect of my being wants to not understand, and so not know (and feel) the horror that the child experienced. And at the same time, I must experience the very pain that the child experienced both when those events were occurring, and later, when the raw memories of those events continued to emerge within his mind and body. I must experience this pain so that the child will not again experience it alone.

Part of me wants to minimize the events, achieve some surface understanding that may lead to some surface relief; rescue the child from them somehow, and convince myself that the events are in the past and the child is safe from them now. What I must never forget is that while I may keep a child safe from experiencing similar events in the present and future, he is not safe from the experience of those past events when they are still so alive within his mind and heart, body and soul. When there are parts of himself – still activated – that drive him into shame and terror, a child is not safe.

As a therapist, I cannot change events. But I can assist a child to face again – with me – the experience of those events, and, in so doing, co-create new experiences, new meanings, and reduce or dissipate their subjective horror.

This small book of poetry and prose is an effort to capture a part of the stories of the children and adults I have come to know over the years by being their therapist, consultant, colleague, and/or friend. These writings reflect my attempts to put into words my intersubjective experiences of the narratives of these individuals who were, and are, having a large impact on my own personal and intersubjective development.

I wrote these poems for myself. Often at night after a day spent with these children and their families. Or after a day trying to help other professionals understand how I experienced the lives of those battling to make a life – to make a self and to make a family. The writing helped me in my own efforts to make sense of these experiences. Who were these children? Who were these parents and carers? Poetry enabled me to reflect emotionally on my experiences. I could not reflect without emotion, or I would not truly understand. I did not think that one day I might have these poems published for others. When Andrea Perry of Worth Publishing heard me read a poem at a conference and, after reading the others, asked me to publish them, I was pleased but a bit worried. Would these poems be able to convey to others what they meant to me? I thought that commentaries might provide a context, and help reduce any ambiguities, and I hope they do.

In short, these poems are my emotional reflections from my professional life with children and families. They helped me to rest and hold myself together when I was working to help children hold themselves together, and help families to come together as well.

It has been years since I was first asked to develop a treatment program for abused and neglected children – 35 years in fact. Providing treatment for these children and their foster and adoptive parents has changed me. I have built a professional life on helping these children to develop a way of living far removed from the way they experienced themselves and their world while they were being given inadequate care. I am confident in saying that many of these children have been able to find such a new way of living.

I am very sad to say that many others were not able to do so. When I was first attempting to assist children who had been traumatized by their parents, I often had the sense that I wasn't helping them at all, and felt very discouraged. One nine year old foster child said that she wanted me to help her to be able to move from foster home to foster home every three months.  One seven year old adopted boy screamed at me that he did not want his adoptive parents to love him.  Many foster and adopted children wanted nothing to do with me.  They didn't want a helpful relationship with me, with their foster or adoptive parents, with their social workers, or with their teachers.

These children not only didn't want such relationships, they didn't know what it was that they were rejecting. They didn't know what they were missing.  They didn't know what babies, born to parents willing and able to care for them and raise them well, discover very early in the first moments of life.  These fortunate infants and young children discover over and over again that what they are discovering about themselves, others, and the larger world is being co-created within their relationships with their parents.  I realized that I needed to be aware of the healthy experiences of a child within a good home, in order to assist a child fostered and adopted because of his traumatic early life, to discover these experiences as well.

Over the years when I entered into the lives of these children and teenagers, a part of them entered my life too.  Whether or not they changed, I changed.  They were having an impact on me.  Sometimes it was their courage. Sometimes it was their rage at the life that they had fallen into.  Sometimes it was their persistence in searching for something different, something better.  Whether or not they changed, I changed by getting to know them.

I began to notice that in giving to them as a therapist,

I was receiving from them. By giving to them I discovered parts of myself that I hadn't noticed before. Or that I had refused to notice. Or noticed because they noticed. And then I began to know one of the reasons why I was able to help them, when I could. They had a positive impact on me and I didn't conceal it. When a child recalled pain from his past, I didn't hide my tears. When a child felt pride in a session over facing his shame with the help of his adoptive father, I beamed with joy. When he recalled his terror, he felt my strong and animated presence that conveyed that we could face that terror – successfully – together.

Gradually I became aware that when children were having an impact on me, I was more able to have an impact on them. Why would that be so surprising? We know that the babies who have a giant positive impact on their parents are the babies who thrive. We also know that the neglected and abused children we work with seldom had any sort of positive impact on their parents. Their parents were the people who were hurting them or ignoring them. Such a baby lost any sense that, at the core of his self, he had the capacity to elicit joy, excitement, warmth, love, and fascination from within the self of this big person, the adult supposed to be caring for him.

So why was it surprising? Probably because in my training, these fundamental human realities – where the greatest development occurs whenever the parent and child are having a reciprocal impact on each other – were either not known or not thought to be relevant. I – and most likely the majority of other therapists and psychologists – had come to believe that our skilful application of therapeutic theory and technique was the main reason why our clients begin to heal and develop. I had not remembered enough that it is within relationships that human beings are able to flourish. The human neurological system was designed for relationships. My greatest influence with a child will most likely exist within the context of the relationship that I have with him, regardless of theory or technique.

This growing awareness of the real meaning of the therapeutic relationship was supported by my increasing knowledge of attachment and intersubjectivity theories,[*] and the bodies of research that support them. These twin theories demonstrate that when the infant is safe in the presence of an attachment figure, the infant's development is best facilitated. When the infant is safe, he or she is now safe-to-explore both self and the world. For the most part, this kind of exploration is not done away from the attachment figure. Rather, it is primarily intersubjective exploration that is both the most interesting and the most productive to the infant. He explores who he is and what the nature of the world is through his experience of his parents' experience of him and the world, along with his direct experience. Thus, both safety and learning have their foundation in the relationship between the infant and his attachment figure.

As the research involving attachment and intersubjectivity continues to grow – and is now supported and enhanced by the emerging research into the human brain – we are aware that what is true for the infant remains true throughout our lifetime. So much so in fact that an important new thrust in the study of the brain is known as Interpersonal Neurobiology,[**] because central components of the human brain are designed for and only thrive within relationship.

As the infant develops and his sense of self becomes organized, it is strongly influenced by the attachment and intersubjective relationship patterns that are being established. This organization of the self, seen over time, can be described as the person's life story – or autobiographical narrative. In the presence of attachment security and rich intersubjective learning, this narrative is likely to become coherent, comprehensive, and internally consistent. The narrative is increasingly unique, while being fascinating, moving, and inspiring to those who know the individual the best. As we more fully experience the narrative of the other, we are able to 'walk in his shoes', and we are likely to do so with warmth, compassion, deep understanding and gratitude for that person's readiness to share his narrative with us.

## About the poems

In the first group of poems – *A Broken Beginning* – I wanted to convey aspects of a child's experience of abuse and/or neglect. This group also includes a child's failed efforts to discover a new life when presented with a new home. The children I think of when I read these poems are most often those who I failed to help. The second group – *A Second Start* – focuses on the fears and vulnerabilities facing children as they begin the journey toward a new beginning. This group of poems includes some that focus on the early stages of this journey, and others that show the final stages where the child is becoming transformed by new family experiences. In this group is one poem that focuses on the experience of an adoptive parent who is trying to raise her child. This poem came to me as I was beginning to understand the depths of pain that parents often experience when they open their hearts and homes to children who reject them.

The third and final group of poems – *Intersubjectivity* – focuses on the experiences of children raised from birth by parents who are able and willing to provide for their developmental needs.   These poems focus on intersubjectivity, a central feature of the relationship within which the child thrives.

This book is a story of hope.   Hope from the many children who are successful in both being able to resolve the abuse and neglect of their past, and then become transformed through a new way of living.   Regretfully, some children are, for a variety of reasons – many of which do not involve them – never able to successfully make the transition to this new life.   Other children never even have the opportunity to leave 'the empty lands' of abuse and neglect.   This book is written for these last two groups of children, in the hope that the poems will serve as one small step in reducing their numbers.   Academic and clinical knowledge is crucial if we are to improve our abilities to assist these children and their families.   The experiential understanding that I hope will come from reading these poems may complement that knowledge.   And, I truly hope it will help to deepen the passion and commitment of our governments, communities, and families to use both knowledge and understanding in making a 'second start' a success.

Dan Hughes 2012

*\* See Glossary, p.124*
*\*\* See the work of Allan Schore and Dan Siegel*

# PART ONE

# A broken beginning

Dan Hughes   It was that one moment

## A broken beginning

For most children, their beginnings are a time of comfort and support, deep interest and discoveries, shared experiences involving warm and gentle eyes and touch. Their brains and hearts are 'designed' to absorb these experiences and to develop in incredible ways and at incredible speed. Their parents want to – need to – care for them with love and sensitivity, again and again.

The beginnings of the children I am writing about are broken. For them, it is hate or indifference, not love. The momentum of their lives has often slowed to a crawl, or even come to a halt. Their brains and hearts did not develop the way they were designed to do. Instead, they developed to survive by relying only on themselves, and the self that had this task was not up to it.

It was easier to write about these children than to be with them. It may be hard to read about them, though I think that we need to do so. They deserve no less.

Dan Hughes   It was that one moment

# Lying among the stones

The indifferent sounds of the orphanage
were not a sweet silence,
but rather stones on my chest
forever causing the hard labor of each breath.

When there is such little rhythm
in one's breathing
and in one's movement
there is little passion to
create a life of meaning
and warmth and joy.

The act of staying alive
takes everything
to find a reason for simply that – simply
pulling and pushing air.

Maybe there is no reason …
maybe a special silence
will come if
I stop the movement of air.
End the mistake that brought me here.
Put this living dirt to better purpose
lying among the stones.

## Lying among the stones

The primary neurological activities of infants involve engagement with their parents in countless, reciprocal activities involving eye contact, joint voice prosody[*] and rhythm, gestures and touch. These activities often begin and end within a split second, yet contain the core intersubjective experience that enables the infant to discover who he is along with the nature of the world he lives in. There are millions of these experiences for the infant, each interwoven into a tapestry that forms the organization of the sense of self.

How different for an infant whose early life is mostly – if not entirely – within an orphanage. When this infant acts to initiate the experience I've described above, nothing happens. When a person attends to him to feed, bathe, or clothe him, the infant is often unable to elicit the reciprocal interactions that create the intersubjective experience of self. The orphanage staff may be caring – but there are just too many babies, not enough staff, and too many different staff for each baby. No-one gets to know the uniqueness of each infant.

Over the years when I provided treatment for a child from an orphanage, I was often struck with how difficult it was for the child to be engaged with me so that he could experience my experience of him. He often would not seem to notice how I noticed him – how he was becoming special to me.  Worse, he didn't seem to be special to himself.  He smiled, talked, ate, and played, but the momentum of life for him was slow.  It was as if he was pushing the days along – yet for little purpose.  It was as if he was not aware of the meaning of his life – the value of his life.

*See Glossary p.125

# So hard to be a child

The cold that will not leave
when under the covers
during the night.

The silence
after the screaming
and hitting and crying
are done.

The sense of
not-touched skin
in the dry air

Not seen,
not held,
not felt
by another

Being called special
by a social worker
while not being
special-to-someone.

A child without parents
makes it so hard
to be a child.

## So hard to be a child

Neglect creates the pervasive sense for the child that she is not safe – that she is all alone, no matter how difficult the present situation is. Beyond that, neglect makes her aware that she is not special enough to have a parent who claims her as her own. Neglect creates a condition within the child that leaves her at risk of experiencing overwhelming rage, terror, and despair throughout the course of her life. And under those raw emotions is the emotion of shame. She is not worth having someone care for her. If she's not worth it, then there is no reason to bother trying, since any new relationship is certain to end in rejection. The new parents will most certainly see what the old parents who neglected her saw.

As therapists and social workers, teachers and residential workers, we often do care for these children, and often are able to see that they are worth caring about. But the child doesn't see this. And if she does, it is only a beginning in her journey toward health. This journey will be very difficult for her to make if she doesn't experience a new parent who cares – who cares deeply and for a long period of time. Who cares still, after she expresses her rage, terror, and despair. Who cares enough to help her to lift her shame.

Dan Hughes   It was that one moment

# invisible

jagged sounds, broken shapes
relentlessly indifferent
without any direction or intention
that might include
who i am.

for the sake of safety i used to
stay away from you
and did not notice your message –
the meaning of your fist.

i am now prepared to care less about safety
just tell me who i am.
please tell me; you must tell me.
even if I am bad, please tell me.

ah, yes! yes!
you tell me that I disgust you
I feel something – pain, much pain.
Yes!  I want the pain!
it is my pain!  It is ME!

let me live within the world of people
rather than outside, unseen.
tell me loudly that I am disgusting
and I, yes 'I', will hold it tightly as truth and
live the meaning of that truth,
clutching it, for I will never –
NO NEVER – be invisible again.

## invisible

If a child had a choice between being abused and being neglected, he would most certainly choose abuse. A child wants to be seen, as do we all. He wants to have an impact on another person, someone who considers him to be someone worth responding to. If he has a choice between having no impact on another person or a negative impact, he will chose the negative impact – he will actively seek 'negative attention'.

Not only will he choose the negative over no impact, but he will even choose the negative over the positive! Why would he do that, when he now has the opportunity to receive 'positive attention'? Because the positive makes him anxious; it doesn't fit his early sense of self, which experienced the earlier abuse or neglect.

So how to help this child realize that he can have a positive impact on good people? We respond to his 'negative-attention seeking' with an accepting, curious, and empathic presence, even while setting a limit. We help him to experience that this 'negative' behavior was his effort to survive abuse or neglect and doesn't reflect his spirit at birth. We help him to know that when he breathes, moves, struggles, notices the leaves, fixes the handle on the lawn mower, laughs during the movie, and plays gently with the dog, we are aware of him, we are pleased and content with him in our presence. We help him to see that having this unique person in our lives, in our home, is a gift to us, regardless of any 'negative behaviors' he is engaged in. And then, slowly maybe, he will start to notice our positive attention and the positive within himself and he will engage in 'positive-attention seeking', and he will accept it.

# Shame

Seen as an object –
an assembly of parts to break –
or worse – parts unnoticed.
I am poorly formed
and I strive to hide –
to be unseen.

There is no value
in the development of the unvalued.

And so I hide.
I live to remain hidden
and to spare the world
the burden I am.

To hide on the earth.
Better yet – in the earth.
To shrink and decay
to not further contaminate
the space reserved
for those of worth.

# Shame

Is this poem a bit harsh? I don't think so. Though it is hard for me to read, still, months after I wrote it. The pervasive shame experienced by children who have been hurt, not seen, or not wanted by their parents is so intense that they often cannot begin to imagine that they contain worth. They cannot imagine that this refers to them: '*No less than the trees and the stars, you have a right to be here*'.*

The temptation – when a child finally speaks her truth, that she is worthless – is to tell her that she is not worthless. This tends to elicit disbelief and increased efforts to convince the parent or professional that she truly is worthless. Our efforts to minimize her sense of shame come in part from our deep sadness over the pain that we see in her over her shame. Our efforts also result from the deep discomfort we experience from the pain that we see in her. We want to rescue her from her shame, and prevent ourselves from experiencing her shame.

What the shame-based child needs from us is the courage and willingness to be with her while she experiences her shame. To have empathy for her shame. To accept its presence and to stand with her when she faces it. Her experience of an adult's love and her commitment to share with him her most difficult moments will do much more to reduce her shame than will any argument or gift.

*Desiderata, Max Ehrmann, 1927*

Dan Hughes   It was that one moment

# I will not listen to your lies

For a time, I don't know how long
but I do know there was a time
when I anticipated that I would be
loved.

And I was puzzled that I was not loved.
Or at least that I was not being loved very well
or very often.

Over time – or it may have been suddenly,
the confusion went.
I knew.
I was not lovable.

Now that I know
I hold this meaning tightly.
There is no other.
I will not listen to your lies.

I may be unlovable
but I am not a fool.
I will not hope for the hopeless.

No, I will not listen to your lies.
I will find a way to disgust you –
it is what I do.
And I will see in your eyes that you do know me now.
and I will hear it in your voice
as you leave.

## I will not listen to your lies

A sad truth of many prospective foster and adoptive placements is that as the child begins to feel safe and wanted in his new home – those very factors that he so wanted at birth – he will become anxious and uncomfortable. Thus, the very reality of progress in the placement makes the placement more and more difficult for the child.

It is as if there is a battle between the child's shame-based perception of himself, along with his fear-based perception of his relationship with his new parents, and the parents' perceptions of him. Can he change his parents' perceptions that he is of worth, before they change his perception that he is worthless? He is terrified of their perception that his view of self is very limited and distorted from how others might experience him. Will the strength that emerges from his terror be greater than his parent's strength, which comes from their love and commitment?

It truly is a battle. Or maybe a better analogy is a race to the finish line. He is desperate to have his parents win, but he will run as fast as he can so that they do not.

# There must be other children

I don't want you to fix me.
I don't like who I am.
So there really is no place
to place your hope.

Don't fix me – break me
into so many pieces that
no parent, no therapist
will even think to waste her time
with the parts that still remain.

Don't comfort me.
There is really nothing to nurture
that deserves to be.
There must be other children
that you can help –
who could use whatever you have.

And don't touch me
with your hands that burn my skin.
It would only cause more pain
if I were to follow you
and begin to hope again.
Never again will I hope again.
Never again.

## There must be other children

Years ago I was often surprised at the intensity of the refusal of abused and neglected children to engage in psychological treatment aimed to assist them in starting a new life.   Initially, I took a non-directive approach, letting the child know that she could focus on whatever she wanted and play with any of many toys or art materials that were available to her.   Most importantly, I was ready and able to provide her with an available, sensitive, and responsive adult – an ideal situation for the child to engage in attachment behaviors with me, or at least, so I thought.

The child would inevitably refuse.   When I gradually took more initiative to gently direct her attention to important areas of her life, she again refused.   When she chose to interact with me, it was to tell me what to do and to have a conflict with me, whether or not I did what she told me to do.

Back then I thought that a traumatized child would want to heal, to resolve the trauma, and to learn how to live a better life.   If she did begin to tentatively allow herself to want these things, her efforts were buried under an overwhelming refusal from deep within her mind and her heart. She would protect the self that she knew, the story that she had created to try to make sense of the betrayal by her parents.   She would fight to maintain a story that people like me were not to be trusted.   The stories that we offered were nothing but tricks, naïve assumptions, or lies.

And so I would try to contradict her story. Again and again I would try to experience her courage and strength, her tiny hopes and dreams for love and joy. I would try to show that I understood why she hated me – and feared me – and I would accept her in her being with me, and hope that she would become confused. All the while I would fight any creeping despair that I might feel over the intensity of her battle. I would try to see that I fought with her to keep her self safe. While hoping that I could help her to see her larger self that contained worth.

Dan Hughes   It was that one moment

# The hardest

My 3rd social worker asked me
when I was eight
what was the hardest
and I spoke of
the spit running off my face
his hand in my shorts
the hate in her eyes.

A few years later
my 4th foster mother
asked the same question
and I replied with
the same answer.

A few years later
my 6th social worker –
or my 8th foster mother –
asked that question again
and I had a new answer.

The hardest is being
asked that question
and finding the answer
written in a report
but not in anyone's
mind and heart.

The hardest is having
no ability, no chance,
to bring meaning and joy
into the life of one person.

The hardest is having
no-one
who will think of me,
wonder about me,
worry about me
after she leaves.

The hardest is knowing
that no-one
laughs or cries
or shares joy or pride
when I do something
that shows something
special about me.

The hardest is being
unclaimed,
to know that I am
not worth claiming.

The hardest is knowing
that there is nothing
unique about me
that would cause one person
to experience me as a gift.

Not one person to experience
my opening heart
and want a place within it.

The hardest is feeling
my heart begin to close.

## The hardest

With many children in foster care, the hardest reality that they face year after year is the fact that no-one wants to claim them as their son or daughter.  While the child protection, foster care, and legal systems exist to meet their best interests, these systems often fail to do so because many of these children still go to bed each night knowing that no-one is really wondering how they are, worrying about them, or looking forward to seeing them.  They are obligations and responsibilities to professionals.  These responsibilities may be taken seriously by dedicated and competent professionals.  But the children are still alone, with a sense of isolation that few adults will ever be able to comprehend.

At the same time though, they are not likely to experience the depth of loneliness that one might expect from being so isolated.  To survive, they have learned to no longer be aware of their loneliness.  They can pretend that they do not need anyone.  While hiding their loneliness from themselves, others do not see it either.  Professionals think that they are 'adjusting well'.  Adults comment that the latest move 'didn't seem to bother him at all'.  They may stop hoping for someone to choose them.  They might even give up the fantasy that someone will someday call them their son or their daughter.

# If my parents had died

If my parents had died
my grief would grip your heart
and you would be with me
and offer your comfort.

They have not died,
though I have lost my
wrinkled, drooling,
cuddling dog
and my blue cap
and my apple tree.

I have also lost parents
I mostly never had,
though I waited for them
to glance, to touch, to hear my whisper.
Please comfort me.

I have lost the hint of a parent
who I sensed because of her occasional smile,
gift,
tied shoelace,
and sometimes warm food.

I do appreciate
your gift of foster care
and your intentions to
give me a beginning.
Please, also, know that I grieve
and offer me comfort.

For what do I grieve?
I grieve over the emptiness
at the beginning of my life.
I grieve over the emptiness
that continues to follow me.

## If my parents had died

Years ago a social worker friend in Maine, Louise Hamilton, spoke with me about the value of training foster parents and social workers to understand and respond to the grief of foster children, just as we train individuals who are hospice workers. Her perspective was that these children are often experiencing intense grief, similar to the grief experienced by children whose parents have died. I thought that her insight was valuable in helping us to respond to the ongoing needs of these children. They are grieving – the loss of their parents – as well as the loss of so much in their lives, including what they never had.

When we perceive children as grieving, we tend to experience significant empathy for them. We immediately focus on their loss and their need for comfort. We immediately see how their loss could be greatly impairing their behavior. We understand more about why they do not seem to appreciate what we give them. We understand their anger and fears, loneliness and sadness. We realize that the fact that they were mistreated by their parents is not a reason for them not to grieve their loss. We realize too, that these children are grieving the loss of their childhood.

So it might be wise for all of us who work with or live with these children, to remember their grief.

# I want my own

I am so tired,
so very tired
of using the mother and father
of other kids
and not having a mom and dad
of my own.

Why don't they understand,
why don't they know that
every kid – every one –
needs his own.
Using someone else's
parents is not the same.

When I'm scared at night,
when my friend ignores me,
when I lose my special pictures,
I want my own.

When I hear a loon call,*
when I have a joke to tell,
when I score a goal,
I want my own.

When I'm hungry or full,
confused or sure,
excited or bored,
I want my own.

My own mom,
my own dad.
I want nothing else.
Please hear me.
I want nothing else.
Just my own mom.
Just my own dad.
Just my very own.

\* *A loon is a water bird of the northern US and Canada that has an other-worldly call at night. I think most US folks would understand how a child would want to share his experience of hearing it with his parent. For children in the UK, it might be an owl. And where you are?*

## I want my own

A number of years ago, I was asked to provide treatment for an 11 year old boy, Jake, who had been in foster care for six years and who had moved four times. I was told by Jake's social worker that his foster parents had told her that Jake would have to move again. His behavioral challenges – while not extreme – were almost continuous. He complained a great deal, never seeming satisfied with anything that they did for him. He often lied about small things, and, once in a while, took something from someone in the family without asking. The foster parents would find it hidden in his room.

Their greatest concern was his apparent indifference to them. They said that they felt that they were caring for a boarder. He seemed to be content with their meeting his physical needs, but seemed to have no interest in their meeting his emotional needs. They didn't feel like they were parents to him. I was asked to assess him and provide treatment, if necessary, to help him to adjust to his new placement and to have more success in it.

Prior to our second session together, Jake had been told by his social worker that he would be moving in a few days to the new foster home, and she had introduced him to his sixth set of foster parents. When I saw Jake he was less animated and inquisitive about my office than in our first meeting. He sat quietly and avoided looking at me. I knew from my experiences with many other children in his situation that if he looked at me, experienced my empathy for him more fully, that he would feel like crying. He did not want that.

I reflected on his having to move again and he replied quickly, and with some intensity, *"I want my own!"* Not knowing what he meant – maybe his birth family, maybe adoption, I replied, *"Your own …?"* Still not looking at me. Then he said, this time with less intensity, *"Someone who will keep me"*. And then he cried.

Permanence – leading to safety, leading to a sense that this is my family, I belong here – is crucial for the development of human beings. Ideally, there is legal recognition of this, whether through birth or through adoption. But a child can also experience this sense in long-term foster care or living with legal guardians, though it can be harder. It is especially hard when the legal system gives priority to the rights of biological parents who are not willing or able to care for him and the foster parents are effectively seen by the system as 'babysitters' or 'childminders'.

Permanence – and the resulting freedom to be a child – comes when the child knows every moment and every day, regardless of what he has done, that his parents will 'keep him'. Jake now has his own.

## PART TWO

# A second start

Dan Hughes    It was that one moment

## A second start

When we give these children what they should have received at the moment of conception, they often have a difficult time using or even wanting our gifts. Their brains had developed to rely on themselves, not parents. Their minds do not imagine that a parent wants what is best for them. The emotion of love is terrifying – as is happiness – as is joy – as is wonder. The emotions of rage, terror, despair are known. They are hard emotions but safe ones, because they are known. So we must begin, and begin again, to make the emotions of love and happiness and joy and wonder known, and safe.

Who is to provide this second start for these children? Not saints, not robots. Living, breathing parents, fallible, imperfect, sometimes exhausted, sometimes – yes, sometimes – parents who themselves begin to slip into rage, terror and despair. We ask a great deal of these parents because they need to do a great deal. We need to ask a great deal of ourselves, those of us who give support and guidance to parents, to ensure that we give them our all – just as they do for their children. They deserve no less.

# You ask why I act as I do

You ask why I act as I do –
My screaming, throwing, hitting –
I think that I should know,
but I don't know.

My actions – they call them
compulsive, impulsive, repulsive –
keep bursting out
of some nameless, chaotic, broken
place that you call my 'self'.

You say that they are intentional,
though I don't know if I've ever had
an intention, if you mean a clear motive
that follows from my own interwoven
thoughts and feelings.
You talk about thoughts and feelings as if I
had any idea what you are talking about.
I guess I have them since you say so but
I just cannot find words – or even pictures –
for them.

If you want to help me …
help me to stop what I'm doing,
you will have to go with me into
the inner place that is me.
You will have to join your thoughts with mine,
your feelings with mine.
Give me words for those moving forms within me.

If I let you discover and name
those inner places in me
I will feel terror that you might
name them 'disgusting' or 'evil'.
Understand why I hesitate.

If you can accept what you find in me
and believe it to be of value
I may learn to do the same.
If you join me inside
and help me to arrange the parts inside –
name, understand, and even be proud of them –
we will know why I do what I do
and we will discover what I now can begin to do.

## You ask why I act as I do

Children who were abused and neglected have great deal of difficulty knowing what they think, feel, or want. They do not have words for their inner lives. As a result, they cannot reflect on their behavior, nor do they reflect well on what things mean to them. It is hard for them to know what they really enjoy, what they want, and what goals they want to develop. When children do not develop this ability to discover their inner lives, they are likely to have less control over their behaviors. They are often at a loss to explain what are described as impulses or symptoms. They have difficulty deciding between alternatives, since any preferences that they have are poorly defined and often not strongly felt.

When children don't know what they themselves think, feel, or want, they are unlikely to know what other children and adults think, feel, or want either. As a result, they often misread others. Given their histories, they are likely to assume negative motives for others' behaviors. For example, a parent may say, *"No, you can't ride your bike because it's time for dinner"*. The child may well think that the parent is using dinner as an excuse. The child may believe that the real reason for the parent denying him his wish to ride his bike is to make him unhappy. Given that assumption, is it not surprising that the child might respond with verbal or physical aggression. But when we ask the child why he became aggressive, he truly doesn't know.

# In our eyes

For so long
I was so sure
that I was bad.

I don't know how many times that
I was kicked,
or the screams – that hurt more than
the kicks –
how many times until I knew
that I was bad.

I learned to deal with being bad.
I didn't need much.
Nothing bothered me.
And then they sent me to
another foster mother – Melinda.
and my earth began to quake.

I want to tell you
how Melinda
made my earth quake.

She saw me, with eyes
so lovely and so painful to look at
when she looked at me
and saw me
like no-one else had ever
seen me before.

She never said that
I was not bad.
No, she never did.
It would have been easy for me
to mock those words.
She never gave me the chance.
My earth would quake
when I showed her
with all the force that I had,
the bad that was in me – and
she saw something different.
She saw sadness, fear, shame,
loneliness –
parts of me that
I did not know were there.
She saw those parts
pushing up into what I did
and she did not name them 'bad'.

More than that,
She was with me
as she saw me and
her earth was so safe, so strong, so warm –
steadying me.

Even more!
The moments when I saw
my tears in her eyes
and felt her tears in my eyes –
her being with me
brought calm to my earth.
The word 'bad' left me
and the sad and fear
and anger and shame
came and went,
came and went,
in our eyes.

More still, so much more …
her eyes, her voice, her touch …
She was so sure about it all.
I'll never know how she knew
who I was and might be.
She stayed with me in my
sadness and shame
and they became smaller and softer –
and other parts of me emerged …
No – they burst from me – joy,
laughter, love, happiness, silliness – and
more is happening too –
I find my little brother's tears
in my eyes.

She still says *"No"*.
Ah!  What a soft *"No"* it is.
She holds me in her heart and mind
when she says it.

There are so many new things
in my mind and heart now.
The old things are still there
but they are new too.
The kicks and scream of my past
no longer scare me
nor make me feel that I'm bad.

So much new to understand,
things that Melinda understands.
That she's teaching me
without books or lectures,
just her eyes, her voice,
her touch.

My earth no longer quakes.
It's solid and green,
windy and warm,
with birds and books
and Melinda.

## In our eyes

Many times over the years, I have seen a child begin to experience her foster or adoptive parent differently. This change often occurs slowly at first, in bits and starts, until it forms a new way of experiencing the parent's experience of the child. And then I notice how the child begins to notice the parent more. The child seems to be hungry to know how the parent experiences her. She becomes almost desperate to know – to know who she is in the eyes of the parent.

This poem tries to capture that internal process whereby the child is trying to rediscover, to reconsider, who she is now, with the experience of her by her foster or adoptive parent as her guide – much like the infant and toddler does continuously. Clearly for this to enable the child to develop a new sense of self with the opportunity for a second start in life, the parent needs to experience the value, the strengths, the goodness of the child. We professionals need to be mindful of our task to support the parent enough, to guide the parent enough, so that she is able to see this child who is there, hidden under the symptoms.

When I am alongside these emerging, delicate, relationships, I experience overwhelming gratitude, sometimes even awe. The child who I know is discovering qualities of himself in his parent's presence that he would never come to experience any other way. Those acts of self-discovery are moments of awakening that I am privileged to witness, and even participate in.

Dan Hughes   It was that one moment

# A prayer of an abused child (recently adopted)

God, I am so confused and so scared …

I even think that you made a mistake with me,

though I don't want to think that – I don't want to.

You either made me to be bad, though I don't know why you would do that.

Or you sent me to live with parents who would hurt me, but I don't know why you would do that either.

So, please forgive me God for thinking that.  I don't know what else to think.


See, now I am living with people who call themselves my parents.

Sandy and Luke their names are

who have not hit me once …

Not once!

Though they might hit me tomorrow

when they find out that I broke their phone,

on purpose because they wouldn't let me call Jim.


How do I believe them?

They say that I'm a good boy!

They don't know much really

don't even know about the bird I killed.

Or how I threw my teacher's purse in the toilet.

Maybe they think the devil did it.

But I know better and you do too.

So I think maybe I should just carry on like I've been doing ever since the
    police came, arrested my dad, put mom in the hospital, took his porn
    and her drugs,
sent me to the
place for crazy kids or bad kids
or both …
like me, I guess.

And Sandy and Luke tell me they love me too.
Like I'd believe that.
Who would love me?
Love is nothing but a trick anyway,
to get you to act good
so the adults' lives are easier.

It was last week the first time I got scared with them.
Sandy was reading me this story and
she put her arm around me.
I wanted to get up and run and I wanted
to lean against her.  So I told her I had to pee.
Later the same day, Luke got excited when I got my bike fixed.
He yelled, *"Yes!"* like I swam across the ocean
and he spun me around
and I laughed
and then I got scared again.
I don't know why I don't like to laugh.

But the worst was yesterday.

Luke let me climb the tree that Sandy always told me not to.

He whispered that we wouldn't tell Sandy.

Then I fell and cut my leg up pretty bad.

Luke carried me into the house.

He held me when Sandy cleaned it up, put this burning stuff on it, and
    put a bandage over it.

I looked at him and he had tears in his eyes.

I thought he must have got hurt too.

He said that he was sad for me.

Sad that I got hurt.

Sad that it was his fault for not listening to Sandy.

He said he was sorry.

And I got scared.

So I don't want to be confused and scared, God.

I haven't been really scared since I got that last beating from my father
    the worst one
where I thought he'd make me swallow the blood but he
just laughed and walked away.

I'm no baby, God.  I just don't get why I'm scared at how Sandy and Luke
    are with me.

Why should I get scared about stuff like that, God?

Why do they treat me that way?

What does it all mean, God?

Why don't you tell me?

I'm no baby, God.

What is true?

Was that true how my parents treated me?

Is this true how Sandy and Luke treat me?

What will happen if I believe that Sandy and Luke are telling the truth and I find out that they are lying?

That is more scary than swallowing my own blood.

Did you send them to trick me God?

Did you send them to say you made a mistake having me born to my parents?

I'm confused God.  Which is it?  Or is it something worse?

Please help me figure this all out and make sense of what I need to do next.

. . . . . . . . . . . . . .

There they are, God, sitting on the couch in the living room like they
    always do after dinner.
They sit close to each other and watch this funny show.
About the only time they seem to be quiet together.

God, they're not sitting close tonight.
There's a space between them
about as big as me.
Sandy's looking at me.
Now she's looking at that space.
And she has her smile.

Thank you, God.
I think I know what this means.
I'm still scared though.
Help me please to get to the couch,
to my seat between them.
I have a long way to go.

## A prayer of an abused child (recently adopted)

Children who are being abused and neglected live in fear, chronic fear.  They never know when they will be hurt next and they do know that there is no place where they will be safe.  They develop defenses against their fears.  One defense that many use is anger or rage.  The intensity of their rage conceals their fear.  Another defense is to run and hide.  When they cannot hide physically they learn to do it psychologically.  They do not think of things, or feel things.  They are mentally and emotionally separate from the events occurring around them.  They become especially good at avoiding fear.

It is a sad reality that often when a child begins to experience good care from his foster or adoptive parents he becomes frightened, even terrified.  They are giving him something that he was so desperate for when he was much younger, and he is terrified to begin to hope for it again.  He is not sure that he deserves it.  He believes that once they realize that he is undeserving, these new people will stop giving him that type of care.  He is not sure that he can trust them.  They might be mean and enjoy tricking him.  In response to the fear, the child often makes it go away by either becoming angry with the new parents or by avoiding them as much as possible – not relying on them, not talking to them, not seeking comfort from them.

Parents need to know about this fear and to be gentle and patient when they provide love that is being rejected. Parents need to maintain hope that what Sandy and Luke were slowly able to achieve, is possible for them and their child too.

# Let me go with you
## (from a therapist)

Since I don't know you
please help me to discover
parts of you that you once
wanted to be found.

I am searching for you
with my voice.
Notice the rhythm of the words
which I hope will convey
that you are safe with me.

I think that you may hide from me
because you expect that I will
turn away from those parts of you
that you believe to be disgusting

You seem to be so sure that you know yourself
so well that you have no doubts about
your lack of worth.
I want to help you to doubt.

You know only what your parents thought
was you and little more.
You stopped trying to know who you were
thinking that they were right −
they were your parents −
how could they be wrong?

They were blind to your hopes
and your dreams.
They did not hear your calls
for safety, nor understand
the meaning of your hand,
reaching for them.
nor why you looked away
and covered your face.

I do not know you,
nor – I believe – do you know yourself.
I know that whatever were their reasons –
your parents were wrong
about who you are.
I know this as I breathe
though I still hardly know you.

So I ask you to
let me go with you
into those hidden parts of you
and we will discover who you are –

Under your fears and doubts
and dark silent emptiness –
with the rhythm of my voice,
the touch of my eyes –
we will – so gently – ever so gently
begin to discover you.

And you will see who I am seeing
And you will see more –
and you will show me –
who you are discovering.
slowly at first,
with hesitation,
then –
with building confidence
and finally – with pride.
Yes.
Let me go with you.

## Let me go with you (from a therapist)

When a therapist begins to provide psychological treatment to an abused and neglected child, she is made aware of his numerous, often severe, symptoms, which are making his life – and the lives of his caregivers and teachers – very challenging. The therapist must slow down and get to know the child. She must get to know who the child thinks he is, who he might be, the meaning of his symptoms, and the meaning of having lived in abuse and neglect.

Just as the therapist must give the child time for this journey of self discovery – a journey that requires that she walk with him – so too must we give the therapist time to gently and persistently come to know who the child is under the symptoms. This is a plea to therapists, to hold the child in mind and heart in a manner suggested by the poem. This child does not need to be – should not be – 'fixed'. He needs to be discovered, as he should have been at birth by the parents who never knew him.

In this poem I stressed the comforting rhythm of the therapist's voice. There is exciting neuropsychological research emerging that demonstrates how a parent's voice, with its modulations and rhythms which convey interest, comfort, gentleness, and care, reduces their child's stress, increases safety, and conveys acceptance and an openness to discovery. A monotone voice, common during a

lecture or from those in a position of detached neutrality,
lacks these important therapeutic qualities.

# Who am I?
## (from an adoptive mother)

Definitely not the person I knew when we adopted Jenny.

I find reasons for not being home when I know that she will be there.

I don't talk about her anymore when I call my sister.

I see Jenny smile – something that used to thrill me to the core of my
    being
and I am cold and distant and skeptical – what does she want?

I can barely breathe when I think about hating
my own daughter.

I shared a bit of this with the therapist I started seeing two weeks ago –
Kathleen – she is an angel who held my hand for a moment at the end.
Accepted my anger
and then my tears.
Not once judging me as I judge myself.

When I think of my old hopes and dreams,
I call myself a naïve fool.
Being a fool is so much better than feeling the pain, unending,
the moment after moment after moment pain
of my grief.

I was so ready to explode if Kathleen
reminded me of my daughter's terrible history.
If she asked me to give her empathy.
But she did not do that
and I was surprised when I began thinking about it myself.

Yes, Jenny was beaten by her father while her mother
screamed at her and said it was her fault.
Yes, she was locked in the basement for
24 hours because she told her father that he was wrong.
Yes, when I think of that I feel a bit of sadness for her –
still – so I don't let myself think about that.

Last week Kathleen gave me some coffee – some coffee!
And I cried for most of the time that I was with her.
And she said hardly a thing.
And I loved her for her few words.

And my husband, John,

did not give me his usual advice this time.
He listened and I think he finally understood.
He said that he did and I believe he does –
and he embraced me with his big arms.

I don't want to understand Jenny anymore.
I'm not interested in who she is.
I don't see any value in playing with her,
talking with her, teaching her to cook.
My God, who am I?

I saw myself as a loving person,
someone who would make the greatest mom
a daughter could ever dream of having.
I saw myself as being warm and giving,
a strong guardian of my child,
a soft nest for my child to curl up in.
Why did she not want the person I was?

When I gave there was no receive
When I laughed there were no smiling eyes gazing at me.
When I touched there was no embrace.
When I talked there was no-one listening.
When I wanted to listen, there was no-one talking.
When I walked in the park, I walked alone.
When I gave her a gift, I found it in the trash.
When I planned a trip with her, she preferred her bedroom.
When I reached for her, she pulled away.
When I sat near her, she left the room.
When I loved her, truly loved her more than I have ever,
   ever, loved a living being,
      she had no love for me.
When I began to hate her
   she hated me in return.

I want to rage, to shout my hatred for all to hear ,
and when Kathleen moves her chair nearer to me,
I can only cry and I don't want to cry.
But I do.
Kathleen gives her mind and heart to me
and I cry.

I awoke the other morning and surprised myself when
I saw Jenny at the kitchen table fixing her bagel.
I'd usually walk around the other side of the table to get my coffee –
This time I walked behind her, bent over and kissed the top of her
    head.
She yelled of course and I did not respond as I got the coffee.
But the surprise was that I was not annoyed inside. I was not tense.
I was not dejected again over the hopelessness of it all.
I just was. I was her mother, she was my daughter.
I kissed, she yelled. That's how it was. That was OK.

What was that about?
Kathleen had a guess but she wanted me to guess first.
It wasn't a guess – I knew.
I was her mother, she was my daughter. That's all.

I have not felt hatred for Jenny since.
Though I've been angry more than a few times.
I still kiss the top of her head, when I can get away with it.
And she yells less.
I still need to cry with Kathleen
And to be held by John.
And I know that Jenny and I will
find a way to be together, mother and daughter.

## Who am I? (from an adoptive mother)

The nature of caregiving consists of the parent caring for her child and her child responding with attachment behavior and/or with enjoyment. When the child does not respond, it becomes increasingly difficult for the parent to continue to care. There is a neurological and psychological basis to this reality. Both caregiving and attachment require a reciprocal response, or they have difficulty continuing.

Many parents over the years have cried and said that they no longer loved their child. They have said that they would continue to raise their child – to meet their commitment to him – but that they no longer experience any pleasure in doing so. This may happen with parents who were poorly cared for themselves when they were children, and their own caregiving behaviors are now weak and easily disrupted during the hard times of parenting. This may also occur when the parent's care does not meet a congruent, reciprocal response. This is most often the case with adoptive and foster parents who have a child who is unwilling – and most likely unable – to experience them as parents and respond positively to the care that they are providing.

I attempted in this poem to convey the experience that I have had of many adoptive parents whose child – overwhelmed by trauma and great difficulty forming attachments – did not respond to them, day after day, year after year. I also attempted to convey this mother's beginning steps toward caring again; tentative, weak, uncertain, but constant once more.

Finally I wrote of one of the most important means that we have to help that parent to care again: caring for the parent. Both her husband, John, and her therapist, Kathleen, did not judge her, tell her what to do, or evaluate her behaviors. They took care of her. By allowing them to do so she came to rely on them, her attachment behaviors were activated; slowly her caregiving behaviors started to return. Attachment and caregiving are indeed reciprocal realities between two individuals, at any age, and within the same individual. Activating the parent's attachment behaviors is likely to activate her caregiving behaviors. Caring for her will facilitate her ability to care for her child again.

*If you are interested in exploring this process in greater detail, I refer you to* Brain-Based Parenting: The neuroscience of caregiving for healthy attachment, *which I wrote with my good friend and colleague, Jon Baylin: WWNorton, 2012.*

# Your sweet persistence

When you brought me to your house
From the empty lands,
I hoped for days with
food, clothes,
not much work,
not too hot, not too cold.
and nights without fear, pain, or touch.

It never occurred to me to want more,
I did not know that there was more.
It was months before I knew enough to know
the real meaning of the empty lands,
and the memory of them became even more painful –
I discovered the pain of discovering what had been missing.

Not knowing love
I was terrified of your love –
thinking that I would no longer exist
if I accepted it.
And then when – not if –
you took it away
I would be nothing.

It was your gentle presence –
your sweet persistence –
in touching me with your smile and voice
and teaching me that these touches were called
comfort, care, compassion, companionship.

It was your loud laugh –
your merry eyes –
that led me from safety to happiness
to rising ripples of joy
that carried me home
and hurled me up among the stars.

So now as I reflect on my life
in the empty lands.
I feel sadness for my unseen self
but not fear or shame.
You – my parents –
finding me and loving me –
fill me with gratitude,
with comfort, and with joy.

## Your sweet persistence

In this poem I attempted to capture the child's need for the small acts of care and love, given again and again, in all varieties of situations and events, if he is to begin to form a new sense of self and a new way of experiencing his family and world. Even when there seems to be a breakthrough, such dramatic changes are likely to result from many, many, much smaller opportunities for change that daily life in a good home can provide.

It is not simply that in his home he is now free from abuse. It is rather that he now experiences what a good home is – a place of safety, laughter, rituals and traditions, singing and crying together, sharing and discovering. And he now knows that he belongs.

# I wanted a mom

I used to be amazed at how the kids at school
would simply talk about going for a walk with their mom
or the pie she baked
or a story she told them at night.
As if it happened every day.

I used to hide my tears from the woman
who was supposed to take care of me.
How they could call that 'care' I don't know.
I hated it when she pretended to be a mom to me
when the social worker came.

Then they said I was getting adopted –
and I'd get two moms.
I just wanted one mom, not two.
What would the other kids think at school?

And mom Beth baked the greatest pies.
And mom Lynn showed me her favorite walk by the pond.
And they both told me stories at night
sometimes together, taking turns
and they did things like that every day.

Sometimes mom Beth would be angry with me – don't forget
I wasn't that good at following the rules and telling the truth and stuff.
When she did get angry
mommy Lynn would give me a hug and stay extra close
until mom Beth and I figured out a way to be close again.
And we always did.

Sometimes I just hated mom Lynn
I just did – like I had to – but I didn't want to and
I didn't know why.
And mom Beth would still bake me a pie.
I couldn't figure that out –
I knew they loved each other a real lot
And when I hated one of them, the other one
still loved me – I could feel it.
And the one I hated still loved me, though
I couldn't feel it for awhile.

Now when I'm at school I talk about my mom
and I'm just like the other kids.
And then I talk about my other mom and the kids are amazed.
I used to want a mom
and now I have two moms.
How lucky is that!

# I wanted a mom

In years past there was more concern about a gay or lesbian couple adopting a child. Reasons for the concern varied from moral issues to the belief that children should have both a mom and a dad. Research is clear now that children thrive when they are in loving, secure homes where there is open communication, habit development, and value given to family life. This is whether the parents are homosexual or heterosexual. The quality of the love felt and communicated between parent and child and between the couple is the important factor to consider. Research is also clear that children are at risk of not thriving when they have multiple homes or group facilities over the years, and lack permanence and attachment security.

I have been fortunate to have gotten to know many adoptive families with two moms or two dads. Their strengths and weaknesses were similar to, not different from, the many other families I got to know that had one parent or had both a mom and a dad. The children who were able to make the difficult journey toward a stable life in a good home tended to have an adoptive parent who was – or adoptive parents who were – deeply committed to them while getting to know and love them and helping them to feel safe and wanted. These were the parents who faced anything in their own attachment history that might make it harder to raise their child. They were also willing and able to develop new parenting skills that were necessary if they were to meet the unique needs of their child.

When assessing which parents had the ability and commitment to provide the child with the home that he or she needed, I realized years ago that the sexual preferences of the parents was not a relevant factor.

# Remembering my father

Following years of seeming indifference
I remembered only my
lack of a father,
not knowing what it might be like to be
my father's son.
Or any man's son.

I could only remember his absence ...
I would not forget his absence
or I would be forgetting
how I fought to organize a self
that contained meaning to me –
though meaning little to him.

And then with trembling voice
and tearing eyes
he spoke to me of his absence.
He spoke to me of his failures in being my father
and he asked for forgiveness.
And I forgave him.

He had not known how a father might be
with his son.
He asked if we might learn together
and I said *"Yes"*.

So my self now is organizing
a space for my father
who is joining me within
our future.

And now my self's past
is organizing a space for him too.
There is now room within my mind
to remember the small times when
he was not absent.
When he told me stories before I slept at night
and took my hand as we crossed the street
and caught a baseball in the park.

In forgiving his absence
I was able to remember his presence
in the past.

Those moments with him –
though not frequent –
make it easier for me
to be present with my own children
and to ask them for forgiveness
for those times when I was not.

## Remembering my father

In working with abused and neglected children over the years, coming to know their past lives and aiding them in the process of developing new lives, I became acutely aware of the power of the parent-child relationship, for worse and for better.  I also became aware of the nature of intersubjectivity, its influence on the developing self, and how new experiences can influence our memory of past events so that we re-experience them and their meaning may change.

In this process I discovered that while these intersubjective experiences with abused and neglected children enabled them to re-experience the abuse from their past, they also influenced me to re-experience my own past.  This poem is more about my own life than the lives of the children I worked with, but I am certain that the same principles apply to theirs.  Intersubjective experiences enable us to time-travel, to go back into the past and have a new experience of a past event.  Through this process – having a new experience of the past event – we often begin to remember other past events that we had forgotten because they did not have a place in the old meanings that we gave those events.

I was stunned when, one day, I was able to accept events involving my father years in the past – his chronic working, silence, frequent absence.  Shortly thereafter I also had the space to remember the positive – how he helped me to fix my bike, played ball with me, and told my brother and me stories before we went to sleep at night. I then realized how much story-telling is central in the work that I do with these children. Going into the past and creating again the stories of our lives carries meaning from the present to the past and back again, and then leads us into the future.

# This one child

As we play and talk
with merry eyes and humming tones,
and I discover this one child
with his freckles and movements and
stories and grins,
and backward hat.

In that moment his soul
is seen with awe and joy
and he becomes warm in my seeing.

And in the next moment this one child
dares to show too
his blackest, deepest bits
of piercing terror
and wandering loss.

In that moment his soul
is seen with awe and compassion
and he stretches into my seeing.

And then this one child
with his one soul
and his flowing smiles and tears,
rests safely in my seeing
as we talk and play.

## This one child

If the treatment of the abused and neglected child is to be beneficial, it is crucial that the therapist discover what is unique about the child. The child must be much more than a diagnosis. More than 'a case'. More than a victim of abuse, or a survivor of abuse.

When an infant is born, the new parent discovers who the infant is. In some cultures, the infant is giving a song that is unique to him, which is sung by his parents upon arriving and departing. The infant discovers what is unique about him because his parents do. He discovers his unique worth, his unique strengths and his endearing features.

The relationship too – between therapist and child or parent and child – is one of a kind. There are subtle variations in how the treatment relationship evolves, in its strengths and weaknesses, in what is shared and explored together, that make the relationship unique. Often the non-verbal characteristics of the dialogue between the therapist and child are what make the relationship the most unique. These non-verbal expressions occur within an attuned state, where the two individuals are resonating with each other, with matched affect, attention, and intentions. These intersubjective experiences do not occur with any other person, and they vary from session to session, even moment to moment.

All of them enable the child to develop a deeper sense of his worth and the unique meaning he holds in the mind and heart of the therapist.

# The belly laugh

That winter day
when I was helping
my adoptive dad,
being nervous of course –
I didn't know that I was,
since I always was –
we were bringing in the
groceries from the car.

The still-white snow
over the ice
rose in the sky,
being drawn up by
my father's rising feet.

He was lying there,
on his back with startled eyes,
surrounded by
celery, bread,
and toilet paper.

I thought to help him,
hoping to stop any
rising rage and so
be safe.

Reaching down
while standing on more
snow over ice
my feet flew too
and I landed on my dad
and the bread, celery, and toilet paper.

Waiting for a scream,
I heard –
I heard a magical,
wonderful, mysterious
sound of laughter.

Dad's body began shaking
and his laughter tumbled and rose
from him to embrace me.
My body began shaking as
I was bouncing with him
and the same sounds came from me
and mixed with dad's
in the falling snow.

I never knew that I had them –
those belly laughs –
until dad called
and they came to him.
I've never been the same since
we found them.

## The belly laugh

While we stress the therapeutic value of helping the child to resolve past traumas and to discover the experience of safety, we cannot forget the importance of the child developing and truly experiencing positive emotional experiences as well. The abused and neglected child may have seldom had the opportunity to experience happiness and laughter, and even less of an opportunity to experience laughter and joy with another person.

This poem also focuses on the positive surprise of this unpredictable event. Abused and neglected children so often want, and need, predictability and structure, since the uncertainties of the past were associated with something bad that was about to happen. When a child is able to be surprised and be open to a possible happy ending to the event, she most likely has been able to establish a degree of safety that leaves her able to experience the positive when it emerges. When she truly gives in to a very special experience – a belly laugh – she has also begun to establish a sense of self that now incorporates the positive.

Dan Hughes   It was that one moment

# Gratitude to an old groundhog

There's no telling
where or when.

For us – my daughter and me – it was an April morning
during our third spring together

I needed a bit of the morning air
out by the pond
with the smells and chill
and sounds of awakening pond life.

She was at my side –
there's a surprise

Without chatter and questions –
an even bigger surprise.

Only the light sounds of the flying insects
And the small splashes of the water bugs.

Until the startle from the bush by the maple.
Most likely it was the old groundhog
or the less likely, less friendly, raccoon.

And her little body leaned into me as she gasped.
And her tiny, soft, delicate, hand clutched at mine
and I put my arm around her shivering, shaking, shoulders
and she stayed.

## Gratitude to an old groundhog

The things that most parents take for granted, the moments of quiet intimacy, of fear and comfort with their children are the same moments that foster and adoptive parents remember so vividly, so much so that when they tell the story of that time, their bodies shiver, their faces beam, and their eyes water.  Without these moments there is no attachment safety and no intersubjective discoveries.  The fundamental realities of what we mean by being a parent or being a son or daughter are based on these unique moments, when our child turns to us as their source of security and in the sharing of wonder.

Foster and adoptive parents dream that these moments will appear in their relationships with their children.  And that their dreams will lead to countless such moments.  And when they do, most likely these parents will never take them for granted.

# Dancing in the light

Her name was Katie
and her name, along with her birth,
her face, and her voice – her cries,
murmurs, and grasping breaths –
were given to her as a curse to life,
leaving her clutching hypervigilance
if she still wanted to breathe.

Alone she lived,
her mind and heart clinging to
solitary connections and beats.

When Jackie entered her life,
this new mother was rejected as
any foreign body should be if
the organism is to live.

Mothers were sharks
ruthlessly waiting while circling for
the mind's energy and the heart's blood.

Fighting sharks may well seem hopeless
but Katie did fight with Jackie
for there seemed to be no other way
to survive.
Until that time when
Jackie ceased to be a shark
and Katie ceased to see herself as a curse.

Jackie did circle for Katie's
mind and heart,
A gentle, persistent, search.
With a face of compassion
A voice of continuous welcome
A touch of strong safety.

It was that one moment,
one similar to thousands of prior moments.
When Katie began to sense,
to know,
to feel-felt in those parts of her
that had never been felt before.

That one moment when Katie knew –
When she dared to know –
when she leaped into her knowing –
that Jackie was discovering some
parts of her, parts
that were gifts to the world,
that needed to be named by her,
to be cherished by her,
to be experienced with
delight and joy
and awe and love –
by her.
Just as they were experienced
by her mother.

And at this point,
when time seems to circle back upon itself.
Katie sees Jackie seeing her seeing Jackie.
She knows that her mind and heart –
actively joining with Jackie's –
will explode in celebrations.
Will beat in rhythms of life
that have moved for mystical generations
from mothers to daughters to mothers again,
dancing in the light.

## Dancing in the light

One of the most damaging aspects of abuse and neglect is that it reduces one's openness to establishing a relationship with an adult, a relationship which is crucial in discovering who one is, and how one is able to have a positive influence on another. One's worth is greatly impaired by the abuse itself. Then, if the child is exposed to a relationship with a caring person, he is less likely to be open to that relationship, even though he is very unlikely to change his negative, poorly defined, sense of self without having such a relationship. Intersubjectivity is the primary source of our social and emotional sense of self and it is greatly compromised when a child has been abused by the first individuals with whom he tried to have such an intersubjective experience.

In this poem I attempted to emphasize how difficult it was for the child to be open to the positive experience that her adoptive mother had of her. Once she was able to be consistently open to such an experience – with a mother who saw her worth, who experienced what was of value about her – then she would be able to benefit from such experiences and re-experience her sense of self.

# I love you

Nobody told me that therapy would be like this.
I had been commanded to talk –
talk about that man –
what fools those people were.
My thoughts, my feelings were mine.
I had no need for others.
I had no need to share –
and then I met you.

How did you know about the soul
that did not need to be fixed?
The spirit that needed to be found,
to be healed
to feel the gentle touch of your kindness
to experience your honest response to my
fears, shame and mistakes.

How did you know about
parts of me that I did not know about?
How did you see within my eyes the
terror, loneliness, confusion
that caused me to hide
what no-one else ever saw?

I thought that you would do your job
and then give up on me.
But then something in me,
in me, IN ME!
would make you smile,
and be worried,
and laugh
and be tender
and silly
and stern
and show tears.
Tears-for-me
for-me FOR-ME!
And I became desperate to know,
truly desperate.
What was this something in me?
What was it!
Who was I!

You are not a mechanic
You are an explorer.
You find treasures where no-one else ever looks
Ah! That is it! Yes! That is it!
I am a treasure to you – though I am so embarrassed
to even think that.
You knew that from the start.
From the start I was becoming a treasure to you!
And your mind and heart continued to know it
though I told you, showed you, screamed to you
that you were wrong
and that it was cruel to tell such lies
and push against my hopelessness
and rage and worthlessness.
And you still knew it
and showed it in your eyes and voice and face
and I somehow –
now – do – too.
I know it too.

No surprise here, after all that you have done for me:
You are a treasure to me!
The buzzing, bewildering miracle is that
I am a treasure to you!

From the bottom and top and middle
of my heart I thank you.
And I know that means something to you too!
My thanking you!
My thanking you helps you to be more of
the incredible person you are!
Such a mystery!
An upside down, inside out,
you-and-me mystery.

And I also know that it means something to you –
I mean something to you –
I am someone to you.
And you are someone to me.
I know this when we cry together
after I put myself in a letter to you
and tell you that I love you.

## I love you

A friend and colleague, Pamela McCloskey, told me of a letter given to her at the end of treatment by an adolescent client. I decided to try to put in writing what I thought many of the adolescents might say who have completed treatment that is based on principles of attachment and intersubjectivity.

Central to the progress is the teen's ability to co-create the story of her life with the therapist actively engaged in the process. Closely related to that theme is the teen's experience of how that joint process of exploration and discovery has such an impact on the therapist. Teens are often amazed that they – and their stories – elicit compassion, deep interest, caring, and then pride and joy within the therapist. They never thought that they could be that meaningful to a good person who is meaningful to them. They did not realize that something unique about who they were would have the power to elicit that experience from the therapist.

This poem is written for this therapist and her young client, now becoming an adult. Their journey together is unique and universal. Whenever two human beings are together, with each fully engaged in the intersubjective art of receiving/giving and giving/receiving, they are as Pamela and her client.

Dan Hughes   It was that one moment

# PART THREE

# Intersubjectivity

Dan Hughes   It was that one moment

## Intersubjectivity

This final section of poems represents my effort to capture the fascinating realities and meanings of intersubjectivity. When an infant is raised in a home where intersubjective experiences are ongoing, that infant's mind and heart develop in very coherent, integrated, and fully functioning ways, in deep reciprocal connections with his parents.

In turn, the act of parenting this infant facilitates very congruent developments in the minds and hearts of his parents. When intersubjective experiences are present, both parent and child develop. When they are absent or seldom present, both parent and child fail to develop well.

Dan Hughes   It was that one moment

# Your moving words

Coming to know you
as your words find me is
much of what makes you
truly unique to me.
Actually, not so much the words themselves,
but how they arrive.

Forcefully, lightly, together, alone,
waves or particles or both.
Approaching, reaching –
discovered, understood.

It is your moving words
that reveal your soul to me.
How they arrive
and how I notice and
welcome them

## Your moving words

This poem attempts to describe the meaning of the intersubjective dialogue between a parent and older child, or between two partners.  The non-verbal components of the dialogue – the facial expressions, voice prosody and rhythm, gestures, and synchrony of these bodily communications – carry the deep emotional and interpersonal meanings of how the two individuals impact each other.  Each such dialogue is unique and each moves the relationship into a deeper place, where both individuals feel better understood by the other, with greater safety and enjoyment in each other's presence.

# With clarity and joy

When you speak to the heart of the other
and the other's heart is touched.
his soul speaks to your soul.

When you talk only to his brain,
your words float away forgotten,
even as they are recorded.
His soul remains silent
and your souls do not meet.

When you help a child
to discover the words
for his life's story,
his heart –
and yours –
beat together
with clarity and joy.

## With clarity and joy

Here I am stressing the dramatic difference between the dialogue when the parent (or partner) gives information to the other – or evaluates the other – and when the intent of the parent is simply to accept and understand the other, which then assists the other to understand the self.

A child needs and values being able to put words to her experience.  It empowers her in developing her narrative and in being able to organize her behavior with her inner life.

Dialogues that convey interest and acceptance to the child are much more likely to elicit the child's full engagement and openness to discovery than are dialogues that convey evaluations and facts.  It is the non-verbal component of the dialogue – the part that is central to the art of story-telling – that touches the heart of the other.  When we give a lecture to someone, we touch only the brain, and often then only the part of the brain that deals with being evaluated. When our words carry – in their modulations and rhythms – emotions and the meaning of our relationship, we touch the other's spirit.

# Moments of psychotherapy and similar relationships

This very moment,
within the expressive movements
of what your mind is experiencing of the past.

I respond and join your expressions –
our expressions now – and I
fly into your past with you.
At your invitation – participating
in your past with you.
Exploring it again, now together,
our minds and hearts.

This very moment,
new meanings are being created
in your past
within the timelessness of
our presence.

This very moment
your flowing narrative
has been changed
by our joining together
within the rhythms of
our feeling and thought.

This very moment 'I' –
having been with you in your past –
has also been changed
by our journey.

This very moment
your new 'self' is present with me
and my new 'self',
is present with you,
welcoming you,
as you welcome me.

## Moments of psychotherapy and similar relationships

The psychotherapist is not able to change the events of the past. However, what the therapist is able to do, with the active participation and open mind and heart of the client, is enter the client's past with him. Then the client, this time with the therapist standing and walking with him, can re-experience those events.

Within this re-experience, the client is often able to re-create the meaning of those past events. Very often, within the act of re-creation, the events lose their associated shame and terror. So the client is changing. Being a part of this process – having the experience of sharing and co-creating the client's experience – the therapist is changing too.

# I will play

If I play with words
forever,
I broaden my understanding of them,
and I become awake
to the realities
that they point to.
Realities that I need to touch
or the words
and realities
will empty.

So I will play forever with words,
and, of course,
I will play forever
without them.

## I will play

Too often in the past, words were seen as the primary way we communicate, in therapy or in the family. Then we became aware how much communication is non-verbal, or − if we are to say what it is rather than what it is not − how much is bodily communication. This important and wonderful momentum may have swung a bit too far whenever words are seen as representing only a superficial, intellectual understanding of realities. I am convinced that the deepest communications often combine the non-verbal and verbal. I am equally convinced that the deepest communications often combine the eyes with facial expressions, along with the joint rhythms of breathing together, with no words in sight. There is no right or wrong here. Just allow the experience to express itself as it wants to do. Sometimes it will need and want words along with the bodily expressions. Sometimes it won't.

# Talking moments

Talking moments with children and other people
Are forms of singing, dancing,
exploring, giggling, attaining,
weeping, wondering, wandering,
within quiet, banging, resting,
bouncing
waving oceans and
clouding brilliantly skies.

They are neither the
lecture, explanation,
reason, nor admonition.
No, no, no!

Talking moments with children and other people
are moments of entering their lives
and welcoming them into ours.

## Talking moments

In much of my activity as a psychologist now, I stress with both therapists and parents the value of PACE in communicating with another person, be they child or adult.

PACE: *playfulness*, with its lightness and confidence; *acceptance*, which never evaluates the person; *curiosity*, which enables one to be open to the other without any assumptions, completely not-knowing; *empathy*, which joins the heart of one with the other.

These four qualities are so obviously present when a parent is engaged with a baby. They have a central place in safe and intersubjective explorations between any two individuals who are engaged in knowing and loving each other. Evaluations of the other's behavior, though certainly necessary in acts of discipline – or teaching – between a parent and child, need to be thoroughly embedded in such an attitude if they are to truly influence the other.

So when a mom uses her stern, evaluating, voice to instruct her toddler not to pinch the cat, she is wise to do so, briefly. Then she immediately follows with her gentle voice, comforting the toddler with empathy over the stress of being corrected, accepting the toddler's desire to play with the cat, and exploring with curiosity ways to play that the cat will enjoy too. This approach works well with toddlers as we help them to become sensitive to other beings.  It works equally well with older children when we remember to use it.

# Being a kid

So much to do –
being a kid –
To make it happen,
to make my world.

When you want to know
my fleeting feelings
that carry my wandering thoughts
and I know that they hold meaning to you –
sometimes delight and surprise
sometimes a quiet being with me –
my flowing awareness
becomes more meaningful to me.

I watch you –
Deeply watch your mind's
flow and bursts and resting times –
and all the events that capture
your living mind.
What I see and am moved by
is so much like what holds you.

With you, I write my story
fashioning the rhythms of my feelings,
developing a world that will
open my mind,
touch my heart,
and hold my soul.

Without your being with me
in my story's creation
it would most certainly
have many gaps.
Being a kid, I have difficulty
creating a world without
experiencing your world
and experiencing
your experience of my
efforts to create mine.

Being a kid
I need to be safely with you.
I need to be in your mind and heart
And have you in mine.

## Being a kid

This poem too stresses the fundamental importance of being with our child, accepting our child, within reciprocal activity and dialogue, to have the greatest impact on our child's development. Too much time is spent with parents evaluating their child, thinking that such cognitive feedback will reinforce good behaviors. Such evaluations (for example, *"Good sharing", "Good using your words", "Good job"*) tend to elicit a somewhat guarded psychological and neurological response, no matter how positive they are.

Is there a place for praise? Praise that has the greatest influence is that which is expressed spontaneously, with emotion, in response to the parent's delight in, excitement about or being impressed by, an accomplishment or act or expression of our child. Praise also has its greatest influence when it is expressed for no other purpose than to express the impact that our child's activity has on us. It has much less value, I believe, when it is expressed with the intention being to reinforce the behavior, to make it happen again.

Our children are very aware of our intentions, thoughts, and feelings related to them. When they experience PACE (*see p.111*) with us most of the time, with limited behavioral evaluations enveloped by PACE, they will discover their story, their spirit, and express themselves in ways that lead to gratitude, joy and resilience.

# Here-and-now-together

Mindfulness is a journey deep into
the here-and-now
where I discover the meanings of the unique tree and rock;
the sounds of the traffic and the birds.

It is the flow of my awareness,
accepting all, even the
moments when I am drifting into there-and-then,
accepting them too, and making them here-and-now.

For me, much of the energy of my mind in mindfulness
comes from within.
The sounds and sights outside of 'me'
often do not come to me enough
to hold me within their meanings.
I know that those sounds and sights –
while being separate from me –
are also parts of me outside my skin
But I forget it.

When I am with another in the here-and-now
where the other is also part of me outside my skin
I do not forget it.
The other's active mind meets me in the present and
holds me.

Together – mindfully together –
our minds focus with ease jointly
and remain here-and-now
with the acceptance, compassion, and curiosity
that leads to awe.

While together
the value and meaning of the here-and-now
is infinitely clear to me
as the rest of time fades
and presence
so vitally sings.

## Here-and-now-together

We are increasingly aware of the positive value of mindfulness in spirituality, health, mental health, education, and the in the art of living well.

Most of the writings and exercises regarding mindfulness and its development focus on the individual mind and ways for it to be aware of and accept the internal and external realities of the present moment. In this poem I am focusing on the activity of mindfulness when it is occurring between two individuals. I believe that intersubjective experiences are, in fact, such a joint activity, and I find that we both experience mindfulness when in such a here-and-now relationship.

# One-of-a-kind

Human uniqueness –
infinite variations
of similar themes
involving waves of
autonomy and connection.

I must discover what is
one-of-a-kind
about you.
And while doing so
give expression to what is
one-of-a-kind
about me.
And in this meeting –
this here-and-now –
one-of-a-kind meeting,
a transforming moment
has been created.

I must express my uniqueness and
experience your uniqueness
if our time together
is to become a conversation
of music and poetry.

## One-of-a-kind

A central feature of intersubjectivity is the joint act of discovering and experiencing what is unique about each other.  In those moments, each is not a category (parent, child, client, therapist, partner, friend) but rather a unique person, unlike any other.  When the moment is truly one of intersubjectivity, the other is not the person she was five minutes ago, or during the last session.  In such moments, each is open to discovering what is unique about the other during this one unique moment.  And then discovering who the other now is in the next moment.  While this idea might be a bit metaphysical – an unrealistic possibility – it nevertheless gives expression to the importance and potential of our here-and-now experience of one another.

# Intersubjectivity

Intersubjectivity is a big old word,
A big philosophical, political word
that warms my heart.

As a new word, a psychological word,
it points to lightness and awe,
excitement and pride,
that we both experience
when our minds and hearts
are joined here-and-now.
It brings along new meanings
with new discoveries
seen together, felt together,
accepted together, and known together,
integrating autonomy and intimacy,
safety and adventure,
self and other,
contained fears and towering joys.

A thanks to Trevarthen and Stern
for bringing this word to us again.
It is a busy word
And needs to be big.

## Intersubjectivity

I wrote this poem and sent it to Colwyn Trevarthen[*]
who in many ways I consider to be a mentor to me.   In
his usual, humble, articulate, Scottish (by way of New
Zealand) manner he was quite clear that philosophers have
spoken about intersubjectivity for hundreds of years.   He
simply studied its presence in the education of the infant,
embedded in the infant's drive toward companionship
with his parent.   Of course Colwyn then went on to share
more of his knowledge with me in his typical generous way.

I thank him for everything I have learned from him, whilst
making it clear that anything I have gotten wrong was my
own doing.

*Colwyn is Emeritus Professor of Child Psychology and Psychobiology
at the University of Edinburgh, and is also a Fellow of the Royal Society
of Edinburgh and a Vice President of the British Association for Early
Childhood Education.   When I first became acquainted with the theory
and research involving infant intersubjectivity that he and his students
have conducted over the years, I became aware of what I needed to know
to begin to reach children who had not been given these experiences in
their early months and years.   Since then he has generously guided me
in my efforts to understand this infant drive to learn in companionship
with his parents.   He has also taught me how to appreciate Guinness and
Edinburgh pubs.
While I have never met Daniel Stern, I have been influenced by his
writings.   I was particularly affected by his book, The Interpersonal
World of the Infant, which was my initial exposure to infant
intersubjectivity.   (Basic Books 1985)

# Glossary

**ATTACHMENT**

refers to the developing relationship between an infant and his caregiver, where the infant prefers the caregiver over other adults and turns to her for comfort and support in times of stress. The child is secure in knowing that any separations in the relationship will be temporary and any problems will be repaired. Failure to develop an organized pattern of attachment will place a child at risk of a variety of emotional and behavioral problems throughout the lifespan. However, if the child or adult is able to develop other relationships characterized by attachment security, this can significantly reduce the risks due to the early attachment difficulties.

**ATTACHMENT FIGURE**

refers to a person to whom one turns for safety, comfort, and support. This may be one's parent, aunt or uncle, teacher, mentor as well as one's best friend or partner as one gets older. Ideally your best friend or partner is your attachment figure (when you need one) and you are his (when he needs one).

**INTERSUBJECTIVITY**

refers to the joint experience between two people in which each is aware of and open to being influenced by the experience of the other person. When a mother communicates love and joy when engaged with her infant, the infant experiences himself as being loveable and enjoyable. When the infant communicates interest and delight when with his mother, the mother experiences herself as being an interesting and delightful mother. The core of an infant's sense of self is his parents' ongoing experience of him.

**MINDFULNESS**     refers to having a mental state where you are both aware of and accepting of all aspects of your experience in the present moment. This creates a relaxed sense of openness to whatever is happening. This awareness might be on a specific feature of your experience, such as your breathing or the sound of traffic, or simply on the flow of experience that is occurring. Such a state tends to promote a variety of psychological and physical benefits.

**VOICE PROSODY**     refers to the non-verbal aspects of the spoken word. This includes the modulations of the voice, the rhythms, inflections, and varying intensities of the words expressed. The major aspect of our emotional communications involve the prosody of the expressed language more than the words themselves. If a person yells *"I'm not angry!"*, we conclude that he is angry but does not want to acknowledge it. On the other hand, when a mother says to her toddler with a twinkle in her eye and a voice of high drama: *"You better not do that!"* her toddler is most likely to know that if he does do it – whatever 'it' is – his mother will respond with playful animation and possibly a joyful chase around the room.

# References

The methods of treatment and childrearing that I have developed to meet the needs of these children and their foster and adoptive parents is called Dyadic Developmental Psychotherapy. These methods have been expanded to assist all families (with whom it is called Attachment-Focused Family Therapy) by using the principles that derive from the theories and research of attachment and intersubjectivity. For a comprehensive presentation of these models of treatment and care, please refer to some of my other writings.

**Golding, K. S. & Hughes, D.** (2012) *Nurturing Confident and Secure Children: Parenting with PACE for children with attachment difficulties* London: Jessica Kingsley

**Hughes, D. & Baylin, J.** (2012) *Brain-Based Parenting: The neuroscience of caregiving for healthy attachment* New York: WWNorton

**Hughes, D.** (2011) *Attachment-Focused Family Therapy Workbook* New York: WWNorton

**Hughes, D.** (2009) *Attachment-Focused Parenting* New York: WWNorton

**Hughes, D.** (2007) *Attachment-Focused Family Therapy* New York: WWNorton

**Hughes, D.** (2006) *Building the Bonds of Attachment* (2nd Ed.) Northvale, NJ: Jason Aronson

**Hughes, D.** (2009) Principles of attachment and intersubjectivity: still relevant in relating with adolescents. In Perry, A. (Ed.) (2009) *Teenagers and Attachment: Helping adolescents engage with life and learning* London: Worth Publishing pp.123-140

**Hughes, D.** (2009) Attachment-Focused treatment for children. In Kerman, M. (Ed.) (2009) *Clinical Pearls of Wisdom* New York: WWNorton pp.169-181

**Hughes, D.** (2009) The communication of emotions and the growth of autonomy and intimacy within family therapy. In Fosha, D., Siegel, D. & Solomon, M. (Eds.) *The Healing Power of Emotion: Affective neuroscience, development, and clinical practice* New York: WWNorton pp.280-303

**Hughes, D.** (2004) An attachment-based treatment of maltreated children and young people *Attachment & Human Development*, 6, 263-278

For further information you might wish to visit:
**danielhughes.org** and **dyadicdevelopmentalpsychotherapy.org**